Life Stories
Christopher Columbus

Roger Grimsby

Illustrated by Peter Dennis

Wayland

Life Stories

Louis Braille
Christopher Columbus
Anne Frank
Gandhi
Helen Keller
Martin Luther King
Florence Nightingale
Mother Teresa

Cover and frontispiece: *A portrait of Christopher Columbus painted a few years after his death. No portrait painted during his lifetime has survived.*

Editor: Anna Girling
Designer: Loraine Hayes

This edition published in 1995 by
Wayland (Publishers) Ltd

First published in 1992 by
Wayland (Publishers) Ltd
61 Western Road, Hove
East Sussex, BN3 1JD, England

British Library Cataloguing in Publication Data
Grimsby, Roger
Christopher Columbus.—(Life stories)
I. Title   II. Series
970.015092

HARDBACK ISBN 0-7502-0477-X

PAPERBACK ISBN 0-7502-1675-1

Typeset by Dorchester Typesetting Group Ltd
Printed in Italy by G. Canale & C.S.p.A., Turin

Contents

Words printed in **bold** appear in the glossary.

Imagine

Imagine a grey ocean. Cold mist swirls over the waves. A line of men and women and children is walking along the beach, towards a new home. It is 25,000 years ago.

Imagine them years later. They have found cave-homes to live in. Imagine their children and grandchildren, and all those who lived after them. They have made homes all over the land: strong tents called tipis and mud-walled houses.

People lived in America long before Columbus thought about sailing across the ocean. They lived in villages like this one.

We call the place they came to America, and the place they came from Asia. They walked thousands of kilometres, long ago, to discover America.

Many thousands of years later, a man from Italy, Christopher Columbus, was living on the island of Madeira, a long way out in the Atlantic Ocean.

Christopher Columbus is his name in English. He also had Italian and Spanish names.

People in Madeira thought there was only ocean to the west, but Christopher Columbus believed there was land.

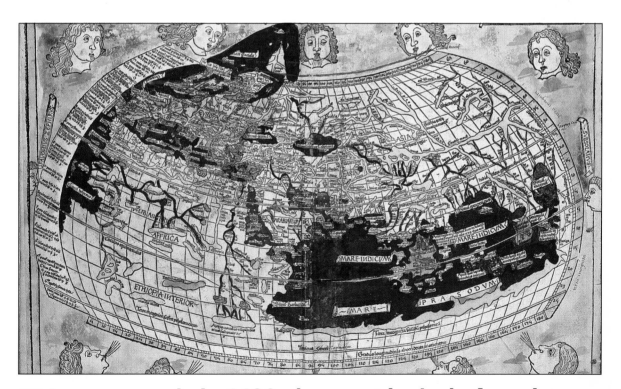

This map, made in 1486, does not include America. People in Europe did not know America was there.

Sometimes the ocean **currents** left objects along the shore. Fishermen brought Columbus pieces of carved wood they found, and strange pine-cones.

One day, the bodies of two odd-looking men were washed ashore, drowned. They did not look like men from the island.

The men whose bodies were washed up on Madeira were probably fishermen from the other side of the ocean.

The bodies, the carved wood and the strange pine-cones were a mystery. Where had they come from?

Columbus thought he knew

Columbus thought he knew. He thought the pieces of carved wood had floated eastward from Cathay (a country we call China). He thought the pine-cones were from trees growing in Cipangu. (We call this country Japan.)

Columbus said: 'Cipangu and Cathay and India are not as far away as people say.'

His dream was to sail westwards to China and the **Indies**. No one believed it was possible. It was too far. In Europe, people did not even know America was there.

In 1486, Columbus journeyed to Spain, to persuade King Ferdinand and Queen Isabella that Cathay and Cipangu, with their gold and **spices**, were waiting over the ocean, to the west. He was going to sail west to the East.

This gold coin shows King Ferdinand and Queen Isabella.

No one believed him. The King of Portugal said: 'Cipangu exists only in the mind of Christopher Columbus.'

Scientists in Spain said the world was much bigger than Columbus thought. (They were right.) He would not find his way across the ocean. (They were wrong.)

A portrait of Christopher Columbus.

This portrait of King Ferdinand was painted in about 1490.

They thought he was a bit mad. They thought he sounded as if he had dreamed it all up.

Then Ferdinand and Isabella changed their minds. The King said he might bring back gold. The Queen said he might make the people of the Indies become **Christians**.

Columbus took small ships like these on his voyage.

Yes, they would help. They would give him three small ships. But he would have to bring back gold and spices. And he would have to make people become Christians.

Columbus agreed. But they would have to call him 'Admiral of the Ocean Sea'. They would have to give him 'a tenth share of all the gold, silver, pearls and jewels that may be found'.

Christopher Columbus was a very proud man. Perhaps he was too proud for his own good.

Columbus' first voyage

Columbus' first voyage began on 3 August 1492. His three ships, the *Santa Maria*, the *Pinta* and the *Nina*, sailed from Spain to the Canary Islands. Then they headed west, into the unknown.

The ocean really was unknown. Columbus did not know which way the winds would blow. He had to guess the sea-currents.

He guessed his men would worry about going so far into the unknown. So he made false entries in the **ship's log**.

'Sunday, 9 September. I made fifteen **leagues** this day but decided to score up a smaller amount so that the crews would not take fright if the voyage were long.'

But on this first journey the ships raced along, often going about fifteen kilometres an hour.

This is a copy of Columbus' ship the **Santa Maria***.*

They had a steady breeze, and a calm sea.

Columbus wrote: 'Sunday, 16 September. The weather is like April in Spain.'

He wrote three or four times that the weather was 'like April in Spain'. He makes it sound like a holiday cruise. But it could not have been.

A ship in those days was a disgusting place. It stank. The food was awful. You often could not find a dry spot to sleep in. If you broke any ship rules you could be flogged or **keel-hauled** or even hanged.

Sailors used the stars to find their way. This sailor is measuring the stars with an astrolabe.

After a month at sea Columbus was looking out for signs of the Indies.

'Monday, 17 September. This morning we saw much more weed, and in it we found a live crab, which I kept. It is a certain sign of land.' (Is it?)

'Friday, 21 September. We saw a whale, a sign that we are near land, for whales always remain near land.' (Do they?!)

But by October some of the crew wanted to go back. They said the sea was too calm! How would they ever get home?

Then they saw land, and the argument ended.

On Friday, 12 October 1492

On Friday, 12 October 1492, two hours after midnight, land appeared.

The Indies! At dawn, there were people on the shore. 'Indians!' thought Columbus. They were friendly. They swam out to Columbus' ship with gifts, one arm high out of the water, holding parrots, balls of cotton thread, wooden spears.

At dawn, Columbus landed on the shore of the island.

Columbus rowed ashore. He knelt and kissed the sand, and claimed the island for Spain. 'I name this island San Salvador,' he said.

Of course it already had a name. Imagine someone kneeling at your front door and saying: 'I name this house Number 32.'

The people crowded round, talking. Columbus thought they were asking: 'Have you come from the sky?'

Columbus had an **interpreter**, to tell him what the 'Indians' were saying, but the interpreter only knew Arabic!

A picture of Columbus' arrival, made in 1494.

The men soon discovered the natural beauty of the islands.

They could not use words, so they tried signs. But the 'Indians' already had a proper sign-language, so even that was difficult. There were soon misunderstandings. Columbus showed them swords but they cut themselves. They had never seen swords.

They could trade

They could **trade** with the 'Indians'. The 'Indians' seemed to want to exchange things. They brought reels of cotton and bits of – ha! – gold…

Soon the 'Indians' were giving their gold away in exchange for any other shiny metal things: little jingly hawk's bells, or the metal points on the men's laces.

It seemed like good friendly fun. But Columbus had ideas that were not so friendly: 'They would be good servants. They would easily be made Christians. I will bring some of them back to the king and queen.'

The people of the Americas were soon desperately running away from the Spanish.

Make servants of them, change their religion, borrow a few to take to Spain...!

Listen to what he wrote to Ferdinand and Isabella: 'Should you command it, all the inhabitants could be taken away to Spain, or made slaves on the island.'

All of them...!

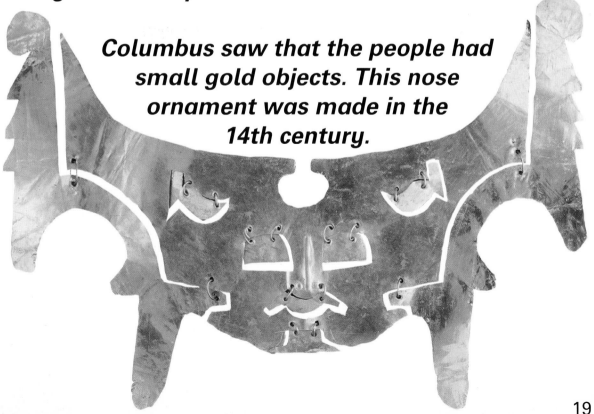

Columbus saw that the people had small gold objects. This nose ornament was made in the 14th century.

Columbus sailed on

Columbus sailed on to find more islands. He gave them new Spanish names – Fernandina, Isabella, Hispaniola and Juana. He said about Hispaniola: 'Here there is a vast quantity of gold.'

Columbus sailed on to many other islands. Can you read the names?

On Christmas Eve, 1492, Columbus' ship, the *Santa Maria*, was wrecked on the coast of Hispaniola.

The crew took ashore all the supplies they could. The 'Indians' from the island helped. Their leader even gave Columbus houses to keep the supplies in.

Columbus thought these people were marvellous: 'There is no better people and no better land in the world. They love their neighbours. Their way of speaking is always gentle and smiling.'

He decided to go back to Spain. He left thirty-six men behind to guard

Hispaniola, in a small fort called Puerto de Navidad – Christmas Harbour.

Off he sailed. He was taking back amazing news of gold and islands. He was taking back 'Indians' too, for the people of Spain to marvel at.

But storms raged, the ships leaked. Many of the 'Indians' died.

A map of Columbus' first voyage.

EUROPE

NORTH AMERICA

THE AZORES

SPAIN

MADEIRA

CANARY ISLANDS

CUBA SAN SALVADOR

HISPANIOLA

AFRICA

CARIBBEAN SEA

ATLANTIC OCEAN

SOUTH AMERICA

N

KEY
Route of Columbus' first voyage

Columbus had returned

Columbus had returned. 'Cathay is only thirty days away by sea!' he said.

The amazing Christopher Columbus! The superstar sailor! Peasants lined the roads to see him pass. **Courtiers** queued to kiss his hand. Rich and poor gawped at the 'Indians'.

King Ferdinand and Queen Isabella wanted him to be off again. They gave him 1,500 men and seventeen ships. The men would build houses and trade for gold.

Columbus left Spain on 25 September 1493, and took only three weeks to reach a new island. He called it Dominica.

They sailed on to Hispaniola, to the fort. They arrived at night, anchored, and lit flares. There was no response from the silent darkness.

At dawn Columbus went ashore and saw why. He found ruined huts, and remains of bodies. The men he had left behind to guard the island had gone off to find gold, and had been killed.

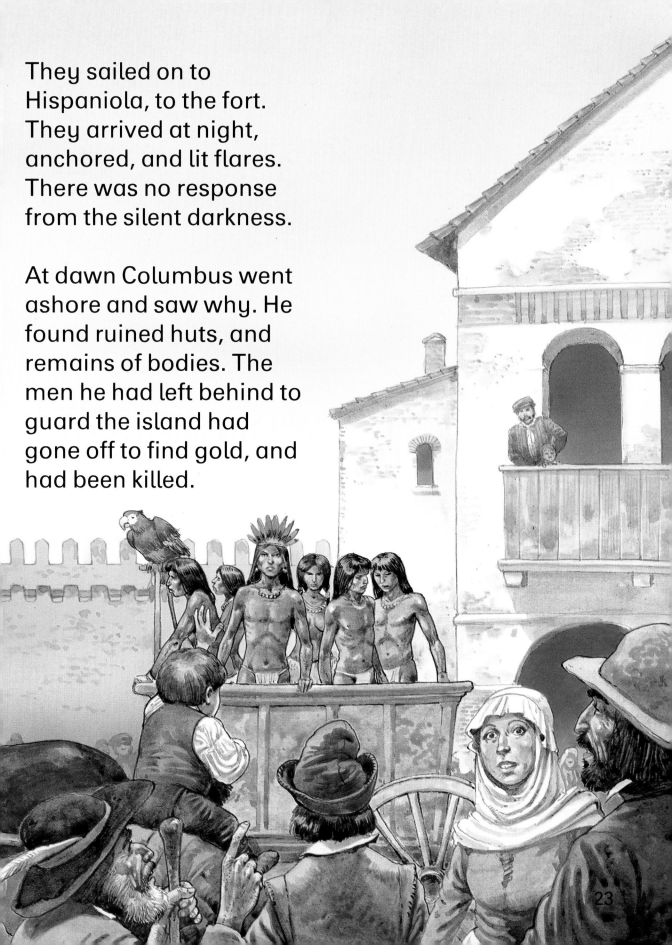

23

A new fort

A new fort was built, called Isabella. Columbus sent a message to Spain. He promised to send gold and spices. There were rich gold-mines on Hispaniola, he said. (There were no gold-mines, only some gold-dust in the rivers.) He said there were **pagodas** with gold roofs, like the ones in Japan. (Of course, there were none.)

They did find riches, but they were nature's riches. They saw beautiful butterflies, flamingoes and turtles.

But gold was even more beautiful, they thought. They needed lots of it to buy supplies from home

– leather, wine, iron. What could they use for money till the gold-mines were found?

Ah...! The 'Indians'! Spanish people would buy 'Indians' to be their slaves! And the money would pay for supplies.

The islands were full of beautiful wildlife, such as flamingoes.

Columbus made up cruel rules. He made the 'Indians' bring him gold-dust. If they did not their hands were cut off.

King Ferdinand and Queen Isabella heard about the cruelty of Columbus' men. Columbus decided to go back to Spain to try and persuade them that everything was well.

But the people of Hispaniola were dying. They died of tiredness in labour gangs, or from being hunted or shot.

There were more than half a million people on Hispaniola when Columbus arrived. By 1548, just over fifty years later, there were only 500. It is hard to believe.

This is an 'Indian' picture of a Spanish soldier. Imagine how the 'Indians' felt about Columbus.

In 1498, Ferdinand and Isabella sent Columbus off to do some more 'discovering'. They were worried that sailors from other places would find land and claim it for their own countries.

This time Columbus 'discovered' the coast of South America. Oddly, he thought he had found **paradise**. He thought he had been sailing uphill, and that the Earth was shaped like a pear!

Perhaps by then Columbus was tired out with all his 'discovering', and a bit mad.

Ferdinand and Isabella sent another man to rule the islands. Columbus was arrested and sent back to Spain in chains.

This is called the Bay of Arrows. When Columbus arrived here he started a battle with local people.

A few years later

A few years later Columbus went across the Atlantic to America for the last time. He found his way through the maze of unknown islands. Then he sailed back with leaky ships to Spain.

In Spain he was not a hero anymore. 'I have no roof to shelter me. When I want a meal or a bed I must go to an inn,' he complained.

When he died, in 1506, no one from court came to his funeral. His death was not even mentioned in the court newspaper.

Imagine a different story. Imagine Columbus asking the 'Indians' what

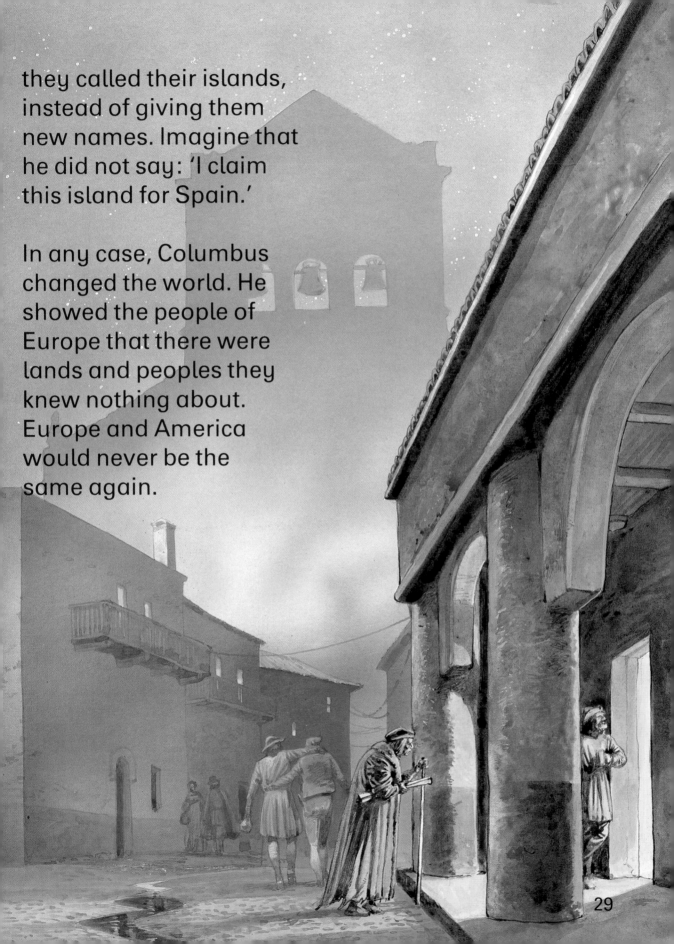

they called their islands, instead of giving them new names. Imagine that he did not say: 'I claim this island for Spain.'

In any case, Columbus changed the world. He showed the people of Europe that there were lands and peoples they knew nothing about. Europe and America would never be the same again.

Glossary

Christians People who follow the teachings of Jesus Christ.

Courtiers People who live in the household, or court, of a king or queen. At the time of Columbus courtiers were rich and important people.

Currents Streams of water that flow in a particular direction.

Indies The name used in Columbus' time for India, China and Japan.

Interpreter Someone who can translate from one language into another.

Keel-hauled Dragged by a rope through the water under a ship, from one side to the other.

League An old measurement of distance. One league is about the same as five kilometres.

Pagodas Decorated temples found in countries in the Far East.

Paradise Another word for heaven.

Scientists People who study nature, the Earth and the universe to find out how things work.

Ship's log A book in which the captain of a ship makes notes about a voyage.

Spices Strong-tasting substances used in cooking to give food a good flavour.

Trade To buy and sell goods.

Date chart

1451 Columbus born in Italy.
1480 Goes to Madeira.
1486 Goes to Spain to ask the King and Queen to support plan to sail west.
1492 3 August Sets off on first voyage.
12 October Sights land.
24 December The *Santa Maria* shipwrecked.
1493 Returns to Spain.
25 September Sets off on second voyage.
1496 Accused of cruelty. Returns to Spain.
1498 Sets off on third voyage.
1500 Arrested and sent back to Spain.
1502–4 Fourth voyage.
1506 Columbus dies in Spain.

Books to read

For younger readers:
The Age of Exploration by Alan Blackwood (Wayland, 1990)
Great Explorers by Tom Jauncey (Wayland, 1986)
See Inside a Galleon ed. R. J. Unstead (Kingfisher, 1988)
For older readers:
The Kingfisher Historical Atlas of Exploration and Empire by Ann Kramer and John Briquebec (Kingfisher, 1990)
The Voyage of Columbus by Rupert Matthews (Wayland, 1989)
The Voyages of Discovery by Brian Williams (Cherrytree, 1989)

Index

Picture acknowledgements
The publishers would like to thank the
following: Bridgeman Art Library 9
(bottom), 14, 19 (bottom); Mary Evans
17 (top), 26; Eye Ubiquitous 13, 25, 27;
Michael Holford 4, 5, 6, 8, 10, 19 (top);
Peter Newark's Historical Pictures 9
(top); Ann Ronan Picture Library 20;
Tony Stone Worldwide 16, 17
(bottom). Map artwork on page 21
supplied by Peter Bull.